Bilingual Edition
My Library of Holidays™
Edición Bilingüe

May Harte
Traducción al español:
Tomás González

PowerKids Press™ & Editorial Buenas Letras™

1

Published in 2004 by The Rosen Publishing Group, Inc.
29 East 21st Street, New York, NY 10010

First Edition

Book Design: Michael J. Caroleo

Photo Credits: Cover and pp. 15, 22 (pumpkins) © Royalty-Free/CORBIS; p. 5 © KJ Historical/CORBIS; pp. 7, 22 (costumes) © Gary Braasch/CORBIS; pp. 9, 22 (Druids) © Adam Woolfitt/CORBIS; p. 11© Nancy Brown/CORBIS; pp. 13, 22 (trick-or-treating) © Joseph Sohm; ChromoSohm Inc./CORBIS; pp. 17, 22 (jack-o'-lanterns) © Philip James Corwin/CORBIS; p. 19 © Joe McDonald/CORBIS; pp. 21, 22 (vampires) © Ed Bock/CORBIS.

Library of Congress Cataloging-in-Publication Data
Harte, May.
  Halloween = Halloween / May Harte ; translated by Tomás González.—
1st ed.
      p. cm. —(My library of holidays)
English and Spanish.
Includes index.
Summary: Provides a brief introduction to the history and current celebration of Halloween.
  ISBN 1-4042-7529-0 (lib. bdg.)
  1. Halloween—Juvenile literature. [1. Halloween. 2. Holidays. 3. Spanish language materials—Bilingual.] I. Title. II. Series.
  GT4965.H35 2004
  394.2646—dc21
                                          2003010277

Manufactured in the United States of America

Contents

Contenido

Every year people have a lot of fun at Halloween. Did you know that Halloween started thousands of years ago in Europe?

Cada año la gente se divierte muchísimo en Halloween o Noche de Brujas. ¿Sabías que Halloween empezó hace miles de años en Europa?

HALLOWE'EN

5

Back then Halloween was called Samhain, which sounds like "SOW-in." People believed that on October 31 the ghosts of dead people returned to Earth.

En esa época a la Noche de Brujas la llamaban *Samhain*. La gente creía que el 31 de octubre los fantasmas de los muertos regresaban a la Tierra.

7

People called Druids lit big fires and wore costumes to scare the ghosts away.

Personas llamadas druidas encendían grandes fogatas y se ponían disfraces para ahuyentar a los fantasmas.

9

When Europeans first came to America, they brought the idea of Halloween with them. Today we dress up in costumes at Halloween just as the Druids did.

Cuando los europeos llegaron por primera vez a América, trajeron consigo la fiesta de Halloween. Hoy nos ponemos disfraces en la Noche de Brujas, igual que hacían los druidas.

We go trick-or-treating. We go to people's doors and yell, "Trick or treat!" We get a lot of candy to take home.

Vamos a las casas a pedir dulces. Tocamos a la puerta y gritamos *Trick or treat!* Eso quiere decir: "¡Dulces o travesura!". Fingimos amenazar a la gente con alguna jugarreta si no nos dan dulces. Esa noche llevamos muchos dulces a casa.

Sometimes we go to places where pumpkins grow and pick them.

A veces vamos a los cultivos y recogemos calabazas.

We can make jack-o'-lanterns by cutting out faces in the pumpkins. We put lights inside to make the faces glow.

Hacemos faroles recortándoles ojos y boca a las calabazas. Les ponemos luces en el interior para que las caras se alumbren.

17

At Halloween we tell stories of vampires that turn into bats.

En la Noche de Brujas contamos cuentos de hombres vampiro que se convierten en murciélagos.

19

Sometimes we dress up as vampires. What will you dress up as next Halloween?

_____

A veces nos disfrazamos de vampiro. ¿De qué te vas a disfrazar el próximo Halloween?

Words to Know
Palabras que debes saber

costumes
disfraces

Druids
druidas

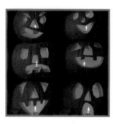

jack-o'-lanterns
faroles

pumpkins
calabazas

trick-or-treating
dulces o travesura

vampires
vampiros

Here are more books to read about Halloween / Otros libros que puedes leer sobre Halloween:

In English/En inglés:
Too Many Pumpkins
by Linda White
Holiday House

Trick or Treat, It's Halloween
by Linda Lowery, Richard Keep
Random House

Due to the changing nature of Internet links, PowerKids Press has developed an online list of Web sites related to the subject of this book. This site is updated regularly. Please use this link to access the list:

www.buenasletraslinks.com/mlholi/hallo/

Index

Índice

Words in English: 165   Palabras en español: 198

Note to Parents, Teachers, and Librarians

PowerKids Readers en Español are specially designed to get emergent and beginning hispanic readers excited about learning to read. Simple stories and concepts are paired with photographs of real kids in real-life situations. Sentences are short and simple, employing a basic vocabulary of sight words, as well as new words that describe familiar things and places. With their engaging stories and vivid photo-illustrations, PowerKids en Español gives children the opportunity to develop a love of reading and learning that they will carry with them throughout their lives.